Keepsake Quilts
for Baby™

Designs by Julie Higgins

HOUSE of
WHITE
BIRCHES
PUBLISHERS
SINCE 1947

Introduction

Patterns for seven heirloom baby quilts that are reminiscent of a gentler, less-hurried time are included in this book. The quilts are designed in softer hues and have a vintage look and feel. These are the quilts that will be passed down from baby to baby's baby. They are almost too beautiful to use.

Personally, I think a quilt acquires the designation "heirloom" based on the complexity of the piecing and quilting. When a quilt includes an abundance of work, it should be appreciated enough to be taken care of. Then there is something left to pass on to the next generation.

Remember the term "Sunday Best?" It simply refers to those things you use on special occasions. I've already made many utility baby and children's quilts, with brights, bugs, animals, etc. I give them to people to use. But here, I wanted to create Sunday-best quilts. These quilts will be going to my baby's babies. I hope they will become their keepsakes one day in the future as reminders of my love.

Meet the Designer
Julie Higgins

Julie Higgins started sewing garments when she was 12 years old. She began making quilts around the year 2000. She has been enthusiastically learning, designing, teaching and speaking to quilters ever since.

Her first book, *Learn English Paper Piecing by Machine*, was released by House of White Birches in June 2005. Her second book, *Creative Fabric Weaving*, was released by the same publisher in February 2006.

Her designs have been published in *McCall's Quick Quilts*, *McCall's Quilting*, *Quilting Arts Magazine*, *Soft Dolls and Animals*, *Quilt Works Today* and *Miniature Quilts*. Her quilt Pauline–She's Got a Good Hand won a Judge's Choice award in the 2006 Indiana Heritage Quilt show. Her quilt Owinja won a Judge's Choice award in the 2003 Miniatures from the Heart Contest. Her quilts have also been juried into the 2003 Hoffman Challenge and 2003 Sulky Loves America exhibits.

Julie lives with her family on the beautiful shore of Lake Lemon, located near Unionville, Ind.

Table of Contents

Dedication

Although this is my third book of designs, I find thankfully that I still have the same people in my life to recognize: My husband, Roger, and our daughter, Becky. I love you both.

Thanks to my friend Jane Pitt, who did the outstanding quilting on two of the projects in this book. It's so nice to be able to say, "Just quilt them however you want to," knowing that they will turn out beautifully.

Thanks also go to my friends in the Bloomington, Indiana Quilters Guild. Your encouragement and friendships mean the world to me. To my editors and the staff of House of White Birches, thanks for making me look good. To everyone that purchased this book— may your quilts always be cherished!

Cats in the Cradle

Stars and diamonds are created when the Cat in the Cradle blocks are pieced and joined in this quilt.

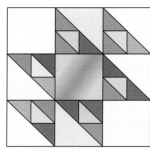

Cat in the Cradle
6" x 6" Block

PROJECT SPECIFICATIONS
Skill Level: Intermediate
Quilt Size: 36" x 48"
Block Size: 6" x 6"
Number of Blocks: 24

FABRIC & BATTING
- ⅓ yard total assorted pink scraps
- ½ yard peach stripe
- ⅔ yard total assorted tan, cream, green and light brown medium scraps
- ⅞ yard total assorted tan and cream light scraps for background
- 1⅔ yards pale yellow floral
- Backing 42" x 54"
- Thin cotton batting 42" x 54"

SUPPLIES & TOOLS
- Neutral color all-purpose thread
- Quilting thread
- Basic sewing tools and supplies

Cutting
1. Cut two 2½" by fabric width strips pale yellow floral; subcut strips into (24) 2½" A squares.

2. Cut (48) 2½" x 2½" B squares light scraps.

3. Cut (72) 2⅞" x 2⅞" squares light scraps; cut each square on one diagonal to make 144 C triangles.

4. Cut (72) 1⅞" x 1⅞" squares pink scraps; cut each square on one diagonal to make 144 D triangles.

5. Cut (216) 1⅞" x 1⅞" squares medium scraps; cut each square on one diagonal to make 432 E triangles.

6. Cut two 2½" x 40" F strips peach stripe.

7. Cut three 2½" by fabric width strips peach stripe. Match stripe and join strips on short ends to make one long strip; press seams open. Subcut strip into two 52" G strips.

8. Cut two 4½" x 40" H strips and two 4½" x 52" I strips along the length of the pale yellow floral.

9. Cut eight 2¼" by remaining fabric width strips pale yellow floral for binding.

Completing the Blocks
1. To complete one Cat in the Cradle block, sew D to E to make a D-E unit as shown in Figure 1; press seam toward E. Repeat to make six D-E units.

Figure 1

Figure 2

2. Sew E to the D sides of each D-E unit to complete a D-E triangle as shown in Figure 2; press seams toward E. Repeat to complete six D-E triangles.

3. Sew C to a D-E triangle to make a C-D-E unit as shown in Figure 3; press seam toward C. Repeat to complete six C-D-E units.

Figure 3   **Figure 4**

4. Arrange the C-D-E units with A and B squares to make rows as shown in Figure 4; join to make rows. Press seams toward A in the center row and away from the center unit in the top and bottom rows. Join the rows to complete one block; press seams in one direction. Repeat to make 24 blocks.

Completing the Quilt

1. Join four blocks to make a row as shown in Figure 5; press seams in one direction. Repeat to make six rows.

Figure 5

2. Join the rows referring to the Placement Diagram for positioning; press seams in one direction.

3. Sew an F strip to an H strip with right sides together along the length; repeat to make two F-H strips. Press seams toward H strips.

4. Sew a G strip to an I strip with right sides together along the length; repeat to make two G-I strips. Press seams toward I.

5. Mark a dot ¼" from the edge of each corner of the pieced center referring to Figure 6.

Figure 6

6. Center and sew F-H strips to the top and bottom and G-I strips to opposite long sides of the pieced center, stopping and securing stitching at the marked dots.

7. Press seams toward F-H and G-I strips.

8. Fold one border strip at a 45-degree angle, starting at the inner seam toward the outer edges referring to Figure 7; press to make a creased line. Fold the quilt at the corner to image the 45-degree angle on the creased strip; start stitching along the creased line at the inner corner of the border strips toward the outer edge as shown in Figure 8.

Figure 7   **Figure 8**   **Figure 9**

9. Trim seam to ¼"; press mitered seam open, referring to Figure 9.

10. Complete the quilt referring to Finishing Your Quilt on page 32. ∎

Cats in the Cradle
Placement Diagram
36" x 48"

Good Morning Sunshine!

Grandmother's Fan blocks in shades of yellow for sunshine and blue for sky are ready to greet baby each morning.

PROJECT SPECIFICATIONS

Skill Level: Advanced
Quilt Size: 38½" x 50½"
Block Size: 6" x 6" and 4¼" x 4¼"
Number of Blocks: 24 and 28

FABRIC & BATTING

- ½ yard medium blue print
- ½ yard white solid
- ½ yard yellow tonal for binding
- 1½ yards total assorted yellow fabrics
- 2 yards total assorted white tonals
- Backing 45" x 57"
- Thin cotton batting 45" x 57"

SUPPLIES & TOOLS

- Neutral color all-purpose thread
- Quilting thread
- Basic sewing tools and supplies

Cutting

1. Prepare templates using pattern pieces given; cut as directed on each piece.

2. Cut two 3½" x 46" G strips and two 3½" x 34" H strips white solid.

3. Cut six 7¼" x 7¼" squares from assorted white tonal scraps; cut each square in half on both diagonals to make 24 I triangles.

4. Cut 1¾"-wide bias strips yellow tonal to total 210" for bias binding.

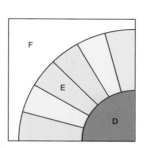

Small Grandmother's Fan
4¼" x 4¼" Block
Make 28

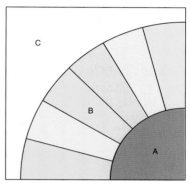

Large Grandmother's Fan
6" x 6" Block
Make 24

Completing the Blocks

1. To complete one Large Grandmother's Fan block, join six B pieces to make a B unit as shown in Figure 1; press seams in one direction.

   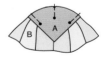

Figure 1   **Figure 2**

2. Pin A to the B unit, matching the notch of A to the center seam of the B unit and placing one pin at each end and one in the center as shown in Figure 2; sew along seam line, readjusting pieces to keep edges aligned and to avoid puckering. Press seam toward A.

3. Repeat step 2 to add C to the A-B unit to complete one block; press seam toward the B unit. Repeat to make 24 blocks.

4. Repeat steps 1–3 with D, E and F units to complete 28 Small Grandmother's Fan blocks.

Completing the Quilt

1. Join four Large Grandmother's Fan blocks to make an X row as shown in Figure 3; press seams in one direction. Repeat to make four X rows.

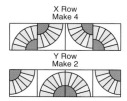

Figure 3

2. Join four Large Grandmother's Fan blocks to make a Y row, again referring to Figure 3; press seams in the opposite direction from the X rows. Repeat to make two Y rows.

3. Arrange and join rows referring to the Placement Diagram to complete the pieced center; press seams in one direction.

4. Center and sew G strips to opposite long sides and H strips to the top and bottom of the pieced center, stopping stitching ¼" from each corner and mitering corners as in steps 5–9 of Cats in the Cradle on page 6. Press seams toward H and G strips.

5. Join six Small Grandmother's Fan blocks with five I triangles to make the top strip as shown in Figure 4; press seams toward I. Repeat to make a bottom strip.

Figure 4

6. Repeat step 5 with eight Small Grandmother's Fan blocks and seven I triangles to make a side strip; press seams toward I. Repeat to make two side strips.

7. Sew the side strips to opposite sides and add the top and bottom strips, joining block seams at the corners to complete the pieced top; press seams toward G and H strips.

8. Use the scallop pattern to mark the edges of each Small Grandmother's Fan block as shown in Figure 5.

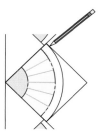

Figure 5

9. Prepare quilt for quilting and quilt as directed in Finishing Your Quilt steps 1 and 2 on page 32.

Good Morning Sunshine!
Placement Diagram
38½" x 50½"

10. Join the bias binding strips with a diagonal seam to make one long strip as shown in Figure 6; trim seam to ¼" and press seams open.

Figure 6

11. Fold under one long edge ¼" and press.

12. Pin and stitch the unfolded edge of the binding right sides together with quilt front

along the marked scallop line as shown in Figure 7, clipping seam allowance at each dip. Keeping needle in the fabric, pivot, realign edges and continue stitching to the next dip.

Figure 7

13. Join binding strips with a diagonal seam at the beginning and end.

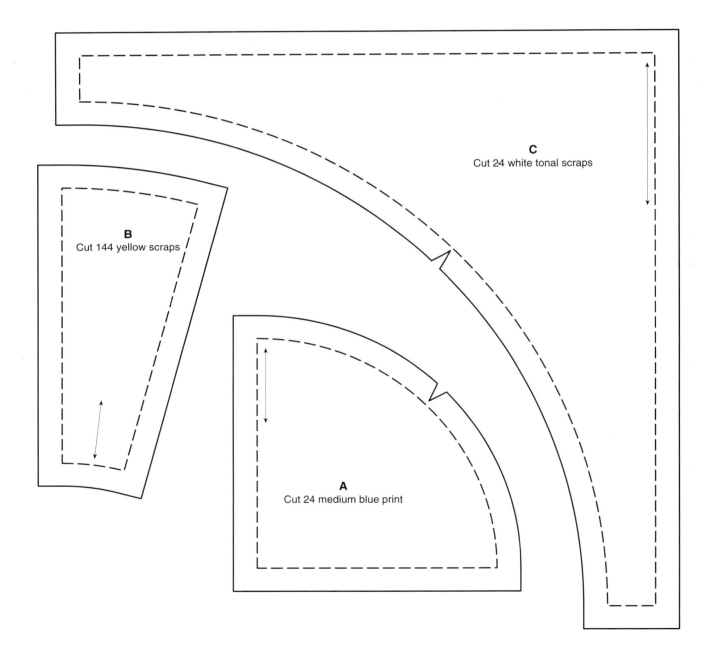

C
Cut 24 white tonal scraps

B
Cut 144 yellow scraps

A
Cut 24 medium blue print

14. Trim batting and backing even with binding seam as shown in Figure 8.

Figure 8

Figure 9

15. Fold binding strip to the wrong side, forming a tuck or pleat at each dip as shown in Figure 9. Hand-stitch in place on the back side to finish. ■

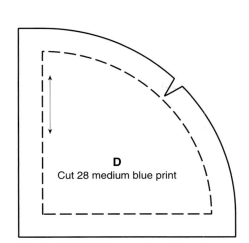

D
Cut 28 medium blue print

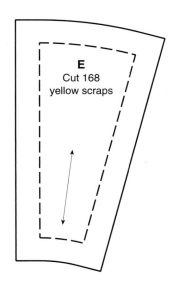

E
Cut 168 yellow scraps

F
Cut 28 white tonal scraps

Scallop Pattern

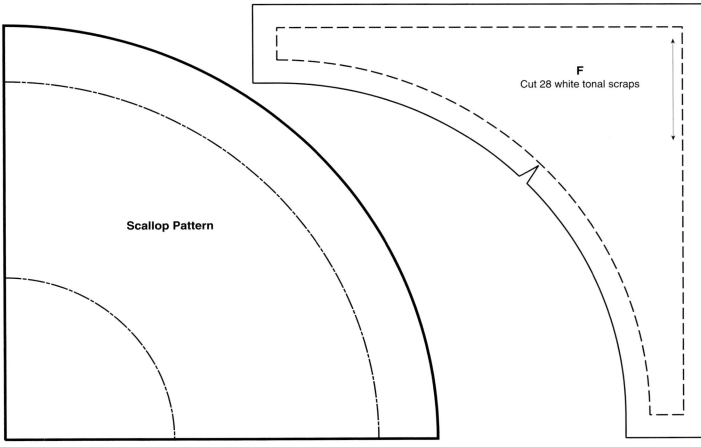

Ribbons & Lace

Create a sweet vintage strippy quilt embellished with lace and ribbons and add a scalloped border.

PROJECT SPECIFICATIONS
Skill Level: Advanced
Quilt Size: 35½" x 44"

FABRIC & BATTING
- 8 (2" x 40½") C strips coordinating prints
- ½ yard cream solid
- ½ yard pink print for bias binding
- ⅝ yard rose floral
- Backing 41" x 50"
- Thin cotton batting 41" x 50"

SUPPLIES & TOOLS
- All-purpose thread to match fabrics and lace
- Quilting thread
- 4 yards lace with ribbon woven through the center
- Basic sewing tools and supplies

Cutting
1. Cut three 5" x 40½" A strips cream solid.

2. Cut four 2" x 40½" B strips rose floral.

3. Cut two 2½" x 40½" D and two 2½" x 36" E strips rose floral.

4. Cut 1¾"-wide bias strips from pink print to total 180" for bias binding.

Completing the Quilt
1. Fold and crease each A strip along the length to mark the center.

2. Cut the lace into three 40½" lengths.

3. Center and stitch a length of lace to each A strip.

4. Join two different-fabric C strips with one B strip with right sides together along length; press seams in one direction. Repeat to make four B-C strips.

5. Join the B-C strips with the A strips to complete the pieced center referring to the Placement Diagram for positioning of strips; press seams away from the A strips.

6. Sew a D strip to opposite long sides and E strips to the top and bottom of the pieced center; press seams toward D and E strips.

7. Use the border templates provided to mark scallops and rounded corners on the border strips as shown in Figure 1.

Figure 1

8. Prepare quilt for quilting and quilt as directed in Finishing Your Quilt steps 1 and 2 on page 32.

9. Join the bias binding strips with a diagonal seam to make one long strip as shown in Figure 2; trim seam to ¼" and press seams open.

Figure 2

10. Fold under one long edge ¼" and press.

11. Pin and stitch binding right sides together with quilt front along the marked scallop line as shown in Figure 3, clipping seam allowance at each dip. Keeping needle in the fabric, pivot, realign edges and continue stitching to the next dip.

Figure 3

12. Join binding strips with a diagonal seam at the beginning and end.

13. Trim batting and backing even with edge of binding as shown in Figure 4.

Figure 4

Figure 5

14. Fold binding strip to the wrong side, forming a tuck or pleat at each dip as shown in Figure 5. Hand-stitch in place on the back side to finish. ■

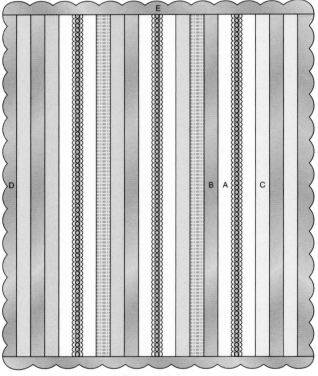

Ribbons & Lace
Placement Diagram
35½" x 44"

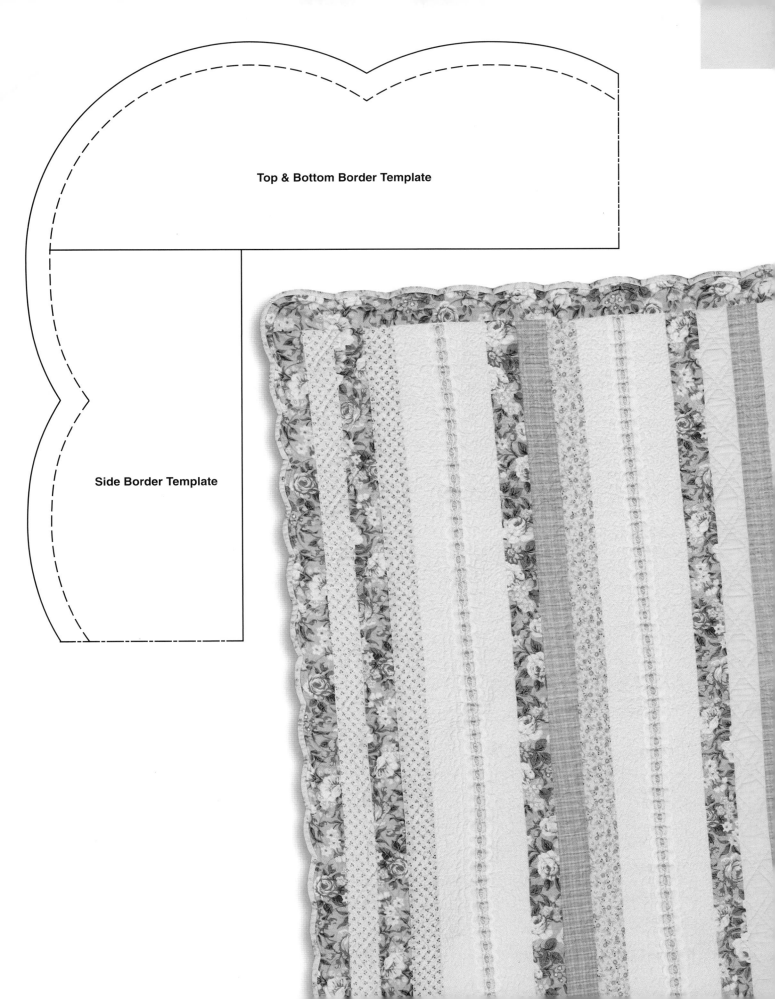

Top & Bottom Border Template

Side Border Template

Grandmother's Diamonds

Lots of vintage or reproduction scraps make this quilt to remind us of earlier days.

PROJECT SPECIFICATIONS
Skill Level: Intermediate
Quilt Size: 38½" x 47⅛"

FABRIC & BATTING
- ⅝ yard blue solid
- 1 yard cream solid
- 1½ yards total vintage or reproduction print scraps
- Backing 45" x 53"
- Thin cotton batting 45" x 53"

SUPPLIES & TOOLS
- Neutral color all-purpose thread
- Quilting thread
- Basic sewing tools and supplies

Hint
Apply spray starch to 60-degree diamond fabrics before cutting to help reduce stretching of pieces during the construction process.

Cutting
1. Prepare templates using patterns given; cut as directed on each piece.

2. Cut two 1" x 37⅝" E strips and two 1" x 30" F strips blue solid.

3. Cut two 5" x 38⅝" G strips and two 5" x 39" H strips cream solid.

4. Cut five 2¼" by fabric width strips blue solid for binding.

Completing the Quilt
1. Join A pieces in diagonal rows referring to Figure 1 and Sewing Offset Seams on page 18; press seams in adjacent rows in opposite directions.

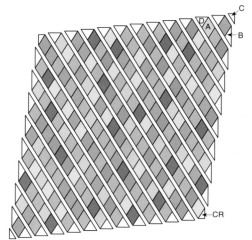

Figure 1

2. Add B, C and D pieces at the ends of rows, again referring to Figure 1; press seams in the same direction as those in the rows to which they are stitched.

3. Join the rows to complete the pieced center; press seams in one direction.

4. Sew E strips to opposite sides and F strips to the top and bottom of the pieced center; press seams toward E and F strips.

5. Sew G strips to opposite sides and H strips to the top and bottom of the pieced center; press seams toward G and H strips.

6. Complete the quilt referring to Finishing Your Quilt on page 32. **Note:** *The wide outside borders are perfect for adding a pretty quilting design.* ◼

Sewing Offset Seams

If you are new to offsetting seams, it takes a little practice to get to the point where you can match seams on sight.

1. When sewing offset seams, you will have little "ears" protruding at each end of the seam line. Even though these 60-degree diamond shapes look like they would fit together just by aligning edges, it does not work as shown in Figure 2.

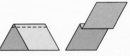

Figure 2

2. Align the pieces so that the V formed at the edge of the pieces will intersect exactly with your ¼" seam allowance as shown in Figure 3.

Figure 3

3. Begin sewing with a ¼" seam allowance as shown in Figure 4.

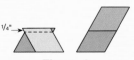

Figure 4

4. Be careful when sewing because 60-degree diamonds have bias edges and will stretch easily.

A
Cut 196 vintage or
reproduction scraps

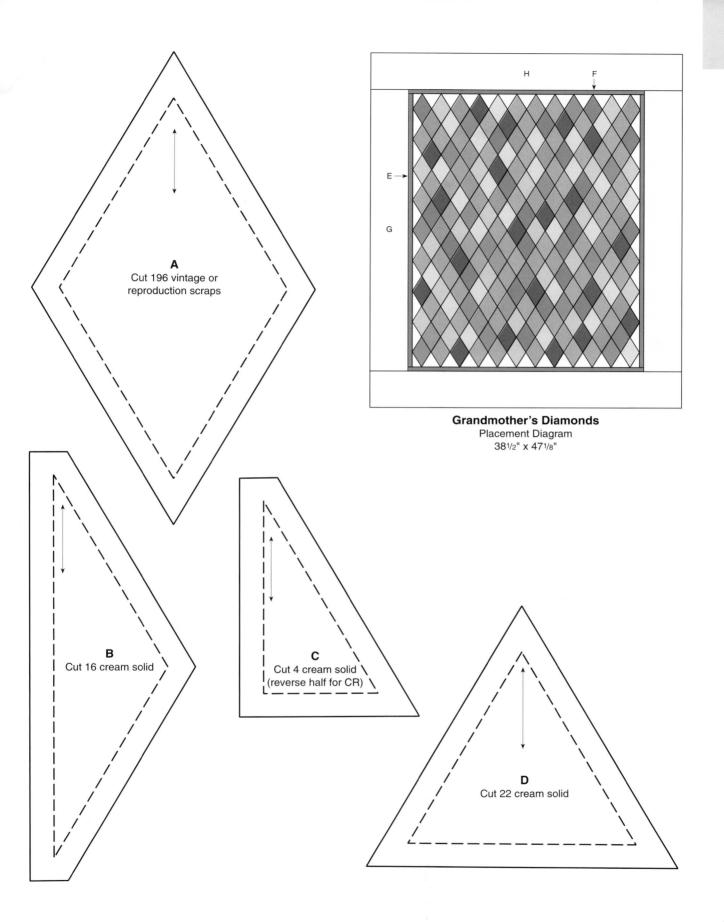

Grandmother's Diamonds
Placement Diagram
$38^1/2$" x $47^1/8$"

B
Cut 16 cream solid

C
Cut 4 cream solid
(reverse half for CR)

D
Cut 22 cream solid

Memories of Nana

Vintage handkerchiefs and lace are used to create a soft and sentimental memory worthy of passing on to a future generation.

PROJECT NOTES

What a wonderful project in which to use that collection of handkerchiefs you have been saving. If you don't have a collection, don't let that stop you. Beautiful vintage handkerchiefs can be found at antique malls, flea markets and yard sales.

Choose handkerchiefs that will make an interesting quilt. These might have lace or crocheted trims, embroidered flowers, etc.

All blocks are pieced with a muslin foundation. They are made ½" larger than needed and are trimmed to size.

Reminiscent of Victorian crazy quilts, this quilt is finished with a knife edge and tied rather than quilted.

PROJECT SPECIFICATIONS

Skill Level: Intermediate
Quilt Size: 27" x 39" without lace edging
Block Size: 6" x 6"
Number of Blocks: 24

FABRIC & BATTING

- 12 or more handkerchiefs
- ¼ yard pale yellow solid
- 1 yard muslin at least 44" wide
- Backing 29" x 41"
- Thin cotton batting 29" x 41"

Crazy Handkerchief
6" x 6" Block

SUPPLIES & TOOLS

- All-purpose thread to match fabrics and lace
- Quilting thread
- Clear monofilament
- Yellow pearl cotton or embroidery floss
- 4–5 yards scalloped cream lace
- 1¾ yards removable fabric stabilizer
- Basic sewing tools and supplies

Cutting

1. Cut four 7" by fabric width strips muslin; subcut strips into (24) 7" foundation squares.

2. Cut (24) 7" x 7" squares removable fabric stabilizer.

3. Cut two 2" x 36½" A strips and two 2" x 27½" B strips pale yellow solid.

Completing the Blocks

1. Select parts of the handkerchiefs you would like to use and layer on top of one muslin square

with finished edges of handkerchiefs covering any raw edges of other handkerchiefs; pin in place. (Photos 1 and 2)

Photo 1

Photo 2

2. Continue adding handkerchiefs to cover the entire muslin foundation. (Photos 3 and 4)

Photo 3

Photo 4

3. When satisfied with the arrangement, rough-cut around the foundation, trimming handkerchief excess. The trimmed block is ready for stitching. (Photos 5 and 6)

Photo 5

Photo 6

4. Pin a removable fabric stabilizer square to the wrong side of the block; sew along the inside edges of each handkerchief to secure in place. *Note: You may use any type of thread with plain or fancy stitches to sew along the edges. If you prefer to showcase the handkerchief edges, use clear monofilament to sew along edges.*

5. When all edges are secure, remove the stabilizer; trim block to 6½" x 6½". Repeat to make 24 blocks.

Completing the Quilt

1. Arrange the blocks in six rows of four blocks each. Join in rows; press seams in adjacent rows in opposite directions.

2. Join the rows to complete the pieced center; press seams in one direction.

3. Sew A strips to opposite long sides and B strips to the top and bottom of the pieced center; press seams toward A and B strips.

4. Place the batting on a flat surface with the prepared backing piece right side up on top; place the pieced quilt top right sides together with the batting/backing layer and pin.

5. Trim excess batting and backing even with quilt top edges.

6. Sew all around edges, leaving an 8" opening on one side; trim corners. Grade seams as shown in Figure 1 to reduce bulk.

| Wrong side of quilt top |
| Wrong side of backing |
| Batting |

Figure 1

7. Turn quilt right side out through the opening, poking corners out to make square; press from the back side.

8. Hand-stitch opening closed.

9. To add lace, place the lace on top of the quilt borders in a pleasing manner; sew top of lace to border strips, extending lace over edges as desired.

Figure 2

10. Tie a square knot in the center of each block and at each block intersection using pearl cotton or 6 strands of embroidery floss as shown in Figure 2. ■

Memories of Nana
Placement Diagram
27" x 39"

Sweet Slumber

What baby wouldn't have the sweetest dreams under this elegant quilt?

PROJECT SPECIFICATIONS
Skill Level: Intermediate
Quilt Size: 42¼" x 50¾"
Block Size: 6" x 6"
Number of Blocks: 18

FABRIC & BATTING
- ¼ yard pale pink print
- ¼ yard pink solid
- ¾ yard light green tonal
- 1 yard medium green tonal
- 1⅔ yards cream tonal
- Backing 48" x 57"
- Thin cotton batting 48" x 57"

SUPPLIES & TOOLS
- Neutral color all-purpose thread
- Clear monofilament
- Quilting thread
- Freezer paper
- Fabric glue stick
- Basic sewing tools and supplies

Cutting
1. Cut three 2½" by fabric width strips medium green tonal; subcut strip into (48) 2½" A squares.

2. Cut four 1½" by fabric width D strips medium green tonal.

3. Cut four 3⅜" x 3⅜" O squares medium green tonal.

4. Cut two 1½" by fabric width L strips pink solid.

5. Cut three 2½" by fabric width strips cream

Appliquéd Flowers
6" x 6" Block
Make 6

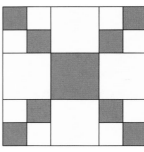

Thrifty
6" x 6" Block
Make 12

tonal; subcut strips into (48) 2½" B squares.

6. Cut six 1½" by fabric width C strips cream tonal.

7. Cut seven 6½" x 6½" E squares cream tonal; fold and crease to mark the diagonal centers of each square.

8. Cut three 9¾" x 9¾" squares cream tonal; cut each square on both diagonals to make 12 F triangles. Two triangles will not be used.

9. Cut two 5⅛" x 5⅛" squares cream tonal; cut each square in half on one diagonal to make four G triangles.

10. Cut two 3½" x 34½" H strips and two 3½" x 32" I strips cream tonal.

11. Cut two 4⅛" by fabric width strips cream tonal; subcut strips into eight 4⅛" squares. Cut each square on both diagonals to make 80 N triangles; two triangles will not be used.

12. Cut one 3⅜" by fabric width strip cream tonal; subcut strip into eight 3⅜" squares. Cut

each square in half on one diagonal to make 16 M triangles.

13. Cut two 1¾" x 40½" J strips and two 1¾" x 34½" K strips light green tonal.

14. Cut five 1¾" by fabric width strips light green tonal. Join strips on short ends to make one long strip; press seams open. Subcut strip into two 48¾" P strips and two 42¾" Q strips.

15. Prepare templates for appliqué shapes using pattern given. Trace shapes onto freezer paper as directed on each piece for number to cut. Cut out shapes on traced lines.

16. Press the waxy side of the freezer-paper shapes on the wrong side of fabrics as directed on patterns for color; cut out shapes, adding ¼" all around as shown in Figure 1.

Figure 1

17. Cut five 2¼" by fabric width strips medium green tonal for binding.

Completing the Appliquéd Flower Blocks

1. Apply fabric glue stick to the ¼" edges of each appliqué shape; turn glued edge over the freezer-paper shape to make smooth edges. Remove freezer paper and finger-press glued edges to the fabric. **Note:** *Do not turn under the edges that will be covered by another piece.*

2. Center two stem pieces on the creased center of an E square referring to Figure 2; baste to hold in place.

Figure 2

3. Place a flower motif at the ends of each stem, layering each motif in numerical order referring to the pattern; baste to hold pieces in place.

4. Using clear monofilament and a machine blind-hem stitch, stitch shapes in place to complete one block. Repeat to make six blocks.

5. Remove basting stitches.

Completing the Thrifty Blocks

1. Sew a C strip to a D strip with right sides together along the length; press seams toward D. Repeat to make four C-D strip sets.

2. Subcut the C-D strip sets into (96) 1½" C-D segments as shown in Figure 3.

Figure 3   **Figure 4**

3. Join two C-D segments to make a C-D unit as shown in Figure 4; press seams in one direction. Repeat to make 48 C-D units.

4. To complete one Thrifty block, join two C-D units with B to make a B-C-D row as shown in Figure 5; press seams toward B. Repeat to make two rows.

Figure 5

5. Sew B to opposite sides of A to make the center row as shown in Figure 6; press seams toward B.

Figure 6

6. Sew the center row between two B-C-D rows to complete one block; press seams toward the center row. Repeat to make 12 blocks.

Completing the Quilt

1. Arrange the blocks in diagonal rows with F and G triangles referring to Figure 7.

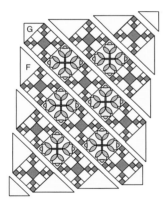

Figure 7

2. Join to make diagonal rows; press seams in adjacent rows in opposite directions. Join the rows to complete the pieced center; press seams in one direction.

3. Sew H strips to opposite long sides and I strips to the top and bottom of the pieced center; press seams toward H and I strips.

4. Sew J strips to opposite long sides and K strips to the top and bottom of the pieced center; press seams toward J and K strips.

5. Sew a C strip to an L strip with right sides together along the length; press seams toward L. Repeat to make two strip sets. Subcut the strip sets into (36) 1½" C-L units as shown in Figure 8.

Figure 8   **Figure 9**

6. Join two C-L units to make a Four-Patch unit as shown in Figure 9; press seam in one direction. Repeat to make 18 Four-Patch units.

7. Sew N to opposite sides of each Four-Patch unit to make an N unit as shown in Figure 10; press seams toward N. Repeat to make 18 N units.

Figure 10

8. Sew one N and two M pieces to A to make a corner unit as shown in Figure 11; repeat to make eight corner units. Press seams toward N and M.

Figure 11   **Figure 12**

9. Sew N to opposite sides of the remaining A squares to make 28 A units as shown in Figure 12; press seams toward N.

10. Join six A units with four N units and two corner units to complete the top row as shown in Figure 13; press seam in one direction. Repeat to complete the bottom row; press seams in one direction.

Figure 13

11. Repeat step 10 with eight A and five N units and two corner units to complete two side rows referring to the Placement Diagram for positioning of units; press seams in one direction.

12. Sew the side rows to opposite long sides of the pieced center; press seams toward J strips.

13. Sew an O square to each end of the top and bottom rows; press seams toward O. Sew to the top and bottom of the pieced center; press seams toward K strips.

14. Sew P strips to opposite long sides and Q strips to the top and bottom of the pieced center; press seams toward P and Q strips to complete the top.

15. Complete the quilt referring to Finishing Your Quilt on page 32. ∎

Sweet Slumber
Placement Diagram
42¼" x 50¾"

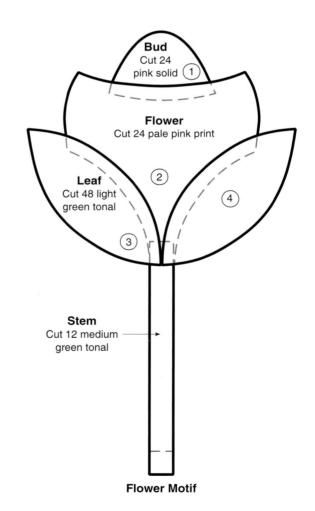

Bud
Cut 24
pink solid ①

Flower
Cut 24 pale pink print

Leaf
Cut 48 light
green tonal

②

④

③

Stem
Cut 12 medium
green tonal

Flower Motif

Little Boy Blues

Blue toile and Civil War-era blues stand out as the center design extends into the border.

PROJECT SPECIFICATIONS
Skill Level: Beginner
Quilt Size: 45" x 57"
Block Size: 6" x 6"
Number of Blocks: 35

FABRIC & BATTING
- ⅝ yard cream tonal
- ⅝ yard dark blue print
- 1¼ yards medium blue print
- 2 yards cream/blue toile
- Backing 51" x 63"
- Thin cotton batting 51" x 63"

SUPPLIES & TOOLS
- Neutral color all-purpose thread
- Quilting thread
- Basic sewing tools and supplies

Cutting
1. Cut three 3½" by fabric width strips cream/blue toile; subcut strips into (32) 3½" F squares. Mark a diagonal line from corner to corner on the wrong side of 28 of the squares.

2. Cut two 5" x 36½" H strips and two 5" x 57½" I strips along the remaining length of the cream/blue toile.

3. Cut three 6½"-wide strips along the remaining length of the cream/blue toile; subcut two of the strips into (18) 6½" A squares and the remaining strip into (10) 3½" G rectangles.

4. Cut six 2½" by fabric width C strips cream tonal; cut two strips in half to make four C half-strips. One C half-strip will not be used.

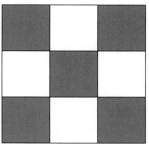

Nine-Patch
6" x 6" Block
Make 17

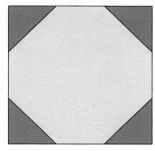

Snowball
6" x 6" Block
Make 18

5. Cut seven 2½" by fabric width D strips dark blue print; cut two strips in half to make four D half-strips. One D half-strip will not be used.

6. Cut five 2½" by fabric width strips medium blue print; subcut strips into (72) B squares. Mark a diagonal line from corner to corner on the wrong side of each square.

7. Cut two 6½" by fabric width strips medium blue print; subcut strips into (14) 3½" E rectangles.

8. Cut six 2¼" by fabric width strips medium blue print for binding.

Completing the Snowball Blocks
1. Referring to Figure 1, pin a B square right sides together on each corner of A; stitch on the marked lines.

Figure 1

2. Trim seam allowances to ¼"; press B to the right side to complete one Snowball block. Repeat to make 18 blocks.

Completing the Nine-Patch Blocks

1. Sew a C strip between two D strips with right sides together along length; press seams toward D strips. Repeat to make two D strip sets; repeat with two D half-strips and one C half-strip to make a D half-strip set.

2. Subcut the D strip and D half-strip sets into (34) 2½" D units as shown in Figure 2.

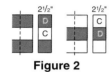

Figure 2

3. Sew a D strip between two C strips with right sides together along length to make a C strip set; press seams toward D strip. Repeat with two C half-strips and one D half-strip to make a C half-strip set.

4. Subcut the C strip and C half-strip sets into (17) 2½" C units, again referring to Figure 2.

5. Sew a C unit between two D units to complete one Nine-Patch block referring to the block drawing; press seams in one direction. Repeat to make 17 blocks.

Completing the Quilt

1. Join two Nine-Patch blocks with three Snowball blocks to make an X row as shown in Figure 3; press seams toward Snowball blocks. Repeat to make four X rows.

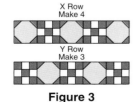

X Row
Make 4

Y Row
Make 3

Figure 3

2. Join two Snowball blocks with three Nine-Patch blocks to make a Y row, again referring to Figure 3; press seams toward Snowball blocks. Repeat to make three Y rows.

3. Join the X and Y rows referring to the Placement Diagram to complete the pieced center; press seams toward the X rows.

4. Referring to Figure 4, stitch an F square right sides together on one end of E; trim seam to ¼". Press F to the right side. Repeat on the other end of E to complete an E-F unit. Repeat to make 14 units.

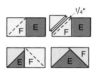

Figure 4

5. Join four E-F units with three G rectangles to make a side strip as shown in Figure 5; press seams toward G. Repeat to make two side strips.

Figure 5

6. Sew a side strip to opposite long sides of the pieced center referring to the Placement Diagram for positioning of strips; press seams toward side strips.

7. Join three E-F units with two G rectangles and two F squares to make the top strip, again referring to Figure 5; press seams toward G. Repeat to make the bottom strip. Sew the strips to the top and bottom of the pieced center referring to the Placement Diagram for positioning of strips.

8. Sew an H strip to the top and bottom and I strips to opposite long sides of the pieced center; press seams toward H and I strips.

9. Complete the quilt referring to Finishing Your Quilt. ■

Little Boy Blues
Placement Diagram
45" x 57"

Finishing Your Quilt

1. Sandwich the batting between the completed top and prepared backing; pin or baste layers together to hold. Note: If using basting spray to hold layers together, refer to instructions on the product container for use.

2. Quilt as desired by hand or machine; remove pins or basting.

3. Trim excess backing and batting even with quilt top.

4. Join binding strips on short ends to make one long strip. Fold the strip in half along length with wrong sides together; press.

5. Sew binding to quilt edges, mitering corners and overlapping ends. Fold binding to the back side and stitch in place to finish.

E-mail: Customer_Service@whitebirches.com

HOUSE of WHITE BIRCHES
PUBLISHERS SINCE 1947

Keepsake Quilts for Baby is published by House of White Birches, 306 East Parr Road, Berne, IN 46711, telephone (260) 589-4000. Printed in USA. Copyright © 2006 House of White Birches.

RETAIL STORES: If you would like to carry this pattern book or any other House of White Birches publications, call the Wholesale Department at Annie's Attic to set up a direct account: (903) 636-4303. Also, request a complete listing of publications available from House of White Birches.

Every effort has been made to ensure that the instructions in this pattern book are complete and accurate. We cannot, however, take responsibility for human error, typographical mistakes or variations in individual work.

ISBN-10: 1-59217-118-4
ISBN-13: 978-1-59217-118-7
1 2 3 4 5 6 7 8 9

STAFF
Editors: Jeanne Stauffer, Sandra L. Hatch
Associate Editor: Dianne Schmidt
Technical Artist: Connie Rand
Copy Supervisor: Michelle Beck
Copy Editors: Sue Harvey, Nicki Lehman, Judy Weatherford
Graphic Arts Supervisor: Ronda Bechinski

Graphic Artists: Debby Keel, Edith Teegarden
Art Director: Brad Snow
Assistant Art Director: Nick Pierce
Photography: Tammy Christian, Don Clark, Matthew Owen, Jackie Schaffel
Photo Stylists: Tammy Nussbaum, Tammy M. Smith

Jane Pitt of Handcrafted Inspirations, Bloomington, Ind., (812) 339-6531, provided professional machine quilting for projects in this book.